PUPPY @ PLAY

Kirsty Seymour-Ure

PUPPY @ PLAY

RYLAND
PETERS
& SMALL

London   New York

First published in the United States in 2002
by Ryland Peters & Small, Inc.
519 Broadway, 5th Floor
New York NY 10012
www.rylandpeters.com

10 9 8 7 6 5 4 3

Text, design, and photographs
© Ryland Peters & Small 2002

Printed and bound in China

ISBN-13: 978 1 84172 290 0
Library of Congress Cataloging-in-Publication Data

Seymour-Ure, Kirsty.
  Puppy @ [i.e. at] play / Kirsty Seymour-Ure.
    p. cm
  ISBN 1-84172-290-1
  1. Puppies. 2. Puppies--Behavior. 3. Puppies--Pictorial
works. I. Title: Puppy at Play. II. Title.

SF426.2.S47 2002
636.7'07'0222--dc21   2001048828

contents

puppy love

Who is not rendered helpless in front of that mixture of wide eyes, flopping ears, out-of-control limbs, and sheer love of life that goes to make up a puppy?

As with the young of any animal, puppies are designed by nature to be cute. Their exaggerated "youthful" traits—the rounded face, the snub nose and big eyes, the baby-soft coat—are literally irresistible to the mother, who responds instinctively to such features. This way, abandonment is guarded against and nurture guaranteed. It is also, of course, these very characteristics that conjure up a similar response in humans and give puppies their great appeal.

PUPPIES POSE

Born unable to see or hear, puppies spend the first few days of life simply sleeping and suckling. But they soon become lively and inquisitive, and after a month or so will be playing actively with their little brothers and sisters. Puppies love company, be it canine or human, or even feline. They adore being the center of attention, where they can indulge to the full their tremendous capacity for friendliness.

amateur amblings

Puppies charm, delight, and win us with their curiosity and love of fun. Even when they are in *big* trouble, we often can't help being secretly beguiled.

SERIOUS FRIVOLITY

Play is a very serious business. Chewing at the carpet, attacking your toes as you sit quietly reading, or mounting a major offensive on the broom as you attempt to sweep: far from being frivolous, this sort of behavior is an essential part of learning what it means to be a dog.

"And puzzling set his puppy brains
To comprehend the case"
William Cowper (1731–1800)

A puppy's sense of smell is very acute from an early age. Without having ever tasted chocolate, a puppy will be sure to find the aroma simply too good to resist, especially if it is combined with the crunchiness and chewability of the tempting cardboard box.

TASTY PUPPY SNACKS

A great many things to eat are enticing to puppies that, later on, they will not deign to touch. Both vegetables and fruit are devoured with the same eager voracity as cookies or cake. Some foods, however, may simply be regarded as somewhat unusual playthings.

25

friends for life

Little creatures with large hearts, puppies love to be loved, and they are boundlessly affectionate in return. Puppies and children are perfect partners.

Puppies and kids are a potent symbol of happiness. They share a zest for living, as well as a talent for fun that is as simple as it is refreshing. Every child should have a puppy to play with, and every puppy should have a child.

TWO FEET BY FOUR

TOGETHERNESS

 For a puppy, there are a few key things that a child cannot do or just isn't good for, and this is where a cat or a kitten comes in handy. In addition to helping to indulge a puppy's investigative urge when the mood is sweet, cats are indispensable as fast-moving objects to chase when energy levels are up. The sight of an enthusiastic puppy barking undaunted at a safe, smug cat high in a tree is a timeless classic.

33

PUPPY PALS

The inbuilt instinct for play and companionship is fulfilled perfectly by the litter. Puppies are born with their natural playmates around them. Be they siblings, friends, or recent acquaintances, a group of puppies will gambol merrily together and can cause havoc in the short space of time that you turn your back to make a cup of coffee.

RUNNING WITH THE PACK

In all their games, puppies are learning the basics of pack behavior and, most importantly, who is the boss. Each puppy has its own distinct personality, and it soon becomes clear who is the leader and who is the clown among them all.

fetch!

Puppies like to chew. They like to bark and wag their tails. They like to jump and leap, to run and to chase. Their joys are simple, honest, and complete.

COULD TRY HARDER

Possessing grace by virtue of their extreme youth and tenderness, puppies are nonetheless clumsy and awkward, as if they haven't yet got used to how their legs work or the ways in which they can manipulate their bodies.

Puppies tend to pounce on just about anything that moves, and on many things that don't. Anything that is chewable, they will chew. Anything that is not chewable, they will still try to chew, just in case. Puppies use their sensitive mouths as

a tool for learning about the world. A tangle of string is useful for exercising the jaws, for developing dexterity, and, no doubt, for practicing a fearless growl.

OUTDOOR PURSUITS

Part of being a puppy is being boisterous, and part of being a boisterous puppy is falling over your own feet, or over the ball a hopeful human has thrown for you. Puppies like to chase balls, but don't expect the ball to be returned to you— they rarely are.

Puppies have fun chasing sticks as well as balls, but they don't bring sticks back, either. They lie down and chew them, in this way combining two basic reflexes in one efficient move. They also enjoy a tug of war with their stick, which is when you find out just how strong your puppy is.

49

Best not to leave your slippers or shoes lying around. A puppy needs to indulge his deep-seated instinct to chew. Luckily, he'll become fond of his own soft toy—a fondness evident from the zeal with which he will chew it up into small, soggy bits.

"His partner in life when he is at home is a pale blue satin bedroom slipper."

Katherine Mansfield

(1888–1923)

ALL CHEWED UP

paws for thought

It's the most enjoyable antics that are also the most tiring. Sleep gives puppies a much-needed refuge from their fast-paced, highly energetic lives.

FLAKED OUT

Mainly, a puppy seems to be a small ball of pure energy, bouncing around the house, jumping up at visitors, gnawing the table legs, and barking at the washing machine. In fact, puppies spend a large part of their time asleep or dozing—vital at the end of a typically strenuous day of being a puppy. Playing hard means resting hard, too.

The innocence of a sleepy puppy's gaze may put us off our guard. Yet never forget that under the guileless exterior, that puppy is quietly gathering energy for another bold assault on the cat, the furniture, or a passing bicycle.

"When he just sits loving and knows that he is being loved..."
John Galsworthy (1867–1933)

Puppies are funny. They have huge feet, uncontrollable limbs, a tail that wags their whole body, and eager smiling faces. They bark wildly at non-existent dangers and run away from the vacuum cleaner. They form ardent attachments to inappropriate objects.

I'M AN ANGEL

They consistently fail to behave in the way the training manual says they will. Puppies have us in stitches, and we love them for making us laugh. When they're sleeping, we see that they are vulnerable. This may be when they're at their sweetest; certainly it's when they are most angelic.

CREDITS

t=top, b=bottom, c=center, l=left, r=right

PHOTOGRAPHY BY:

Chris Tubbs 1, 4-5, 13 **tl**, 13 **tcl**, 13 **br**, 14, 22-23, 34-35, 38, 44-47, 62

Lena Ikse Bergman 6, 10-12, 17, 18-19, 24-25, 29, 30-31, 54, 61

Chris Everard front jacket, 2, 3, 9, 13 **bl**, 13 **tcr**, 13 **tr**, 20-21, 26, 32-33, 36-37, 41-43, 48-52, 56-59, 64, endpapers front and back

The publisher would like to thank
everyone who allowed us to
photograph their puppies:
René Snyder, Elspeth Thompson,
Lucie Neale, Chris London, Lydia Lees,
Kirsty Fitzgerald, Ros Morgan, Martin,
Deborah Corrigan, Melony Collins,
and Lara Beydoun.

Thanks also to trainers Catherine
Madden t. +44 20 7350 2647,
Jon Harte, Dog Hollow Canine
Welfare and Education
t. +44 20 7703 4854, and
Patricia Sears t. +44 20 8995 3092.

Special thanks to the Guide Dogs for
the Blind Association for allowing us
to photograph some of their puppies.